KU-655-554

Crystals

Melissa Stewart

Heinemann
LIBRARY

www.heinemann.co.uk/library
Visit our website to find out more information about Heinemann Library books.

To order:
☎ Phone 44 (0) 1865 888066
▤ Send a fax to 44 (0) 1865 314091
▢ Visit the Heinemann Bookshop at www.heinemann.co.uk/library to browse our catalogue and order online.

First published in Great Britain by Heinemann Library, Halley Court, Jordan Hill, Oxford OX2 8EJ
a division of Reed Educational and Professional Publishing Ltd. Heinemann is a registered trademark
of Reed Educational and Professional Publishing Ltd.

OXFORD MELBOURNE AUCKLAND JOHANNESBURG BLANTYRE
GABORONE IBADAN PORTSMOUTH (NH) USA CHICAGO

© Reed Educational and Professional Publishing Ltd 2002
The moral right of the proprietor has been asserted.

All rights reserved. No part of this publication may be reproduced, stored in a retrieval system, or transmitted
in any form or by any means, electronic, mechanical, photocopying, recording, or otherwise without either the
prior written permission of the Publishers or a licence permitting restricted copying in the United Kingdom
issued by the Copyright Licensing Agency Ltd, 90 Tottenham Court Road, London W1P 0LP.

Produced for Heinemann Library by Editorial Directions
Designed by Ox and Company
Originated by Ambassador Litho Ltd
Printed in Hong Kong

ISBN 0 431 14370 6
06 05 04 03 02
10 9 8 7 6 5 4 3 2 1

British Library Cataloguing in Publication Data
Stewart, Melissa
    Crystals. – (Rocks and minerals)
    1. Crystals – Juvenile literature
    I. Title
    548

Acknowledgements
The Publishers would like to thank the following for permission to reproduce photographs:

Photographs ©: Cover background, Brian Parker/Tom Stack & Associates; cover foreground, Mark A. Schneider/Visuals
Unlimited, Inc.; p. 4, Gamma Liaison/Hulton/Archive; p. 5 Jose Manuel Sanchis Calvete/Corbis; p. 6 Tom & Therisa
Stack/Tom Stack & Associates; p.7 S.K. Mittwede/Visuals Unlimited, Inc.; p. 8 Roberto de Gugliemo/Science Photo
Library/Photo Researchers, Inc.; pp. 9, 10 Mark A. Schneider/Visuals Unlimited, Inc.; p. 11 Ken Lucas/Visuals Unlimited,
Inc.; p. 13, Joe Carini/The Image Works; p. 14 Jeff J. Daly/Visuals Unlimited, Inc.; p. 15 Gary Milburn/Tom Stack &
Associates; p. 16 Prism Rogers/Martin/FPG International; p. 17 Ken Lucas/Visuals Unlimited, Inc.; p. 18 top A.J.
Copley/Visuals Unlimited, Inc.; p. 18 bottom Arthur Hill/Visuals Unlimited, Inc.; p. 19 Grace Davies Photography; p. 20
Cameramann International, Ltd.; p. 21 Volker Steger/Science Photo Library/Photo Researchers, Inc.; p. 22 Allen B.
Smith/Tom Stack & Associates; p. 23 Ken Lucas/Visuals Unlimited, Inc.; p. 24 William J. Weber/Visuals Unlimited, Inc.;
p. 25 Cabisco/Visuals Unlimited, Inc.; p. 26 Allen B. Smith/Tom Stack & Associates; pp. 27, 28, 29 A.J. Copley/Visuals
Unlimited, Inc.

Every effort has been made to contact copyright holders of any material reproduced in this book. Any omissions will be
rectified in subsequent printings if notice is given to the Publishers.

Our thanks to Alan Timms and Martin Lawrence of the Natural History Museum, London for their assistance in the
preparation of this edition.

Disclaimer
All the Internet addresses (URLs) given in this book were valid at the time of going to press. However, due to the dynamic
nature of the Internet, some addresses may have changed, or sites may have changed or ceased to exist since publication.
While the author and Publishers regret any inconvenience this may cause readers, no responsibility for any such changes can
be accepted by either the author or the Publishers.

Contents

Any words appearing in the text in bold, **like this**, are explained in the Glossary.

What is a crystal?

What does a sparkling diamond have in common with a snowflake and the salt you sprinkle on your food? They are all crystals. A crystal is a natural solid made of **atoms** that are always arranged in the same way. If no outside force acts on a crystal as it forms, it will have a regular shape and smooth, flat sides called **faces**.

Salt and snow

Some crystals contain only one kind of atom. For example, a diamond is made entirely of carbon atoms. Most crystals contain two or more kinds of atoms. Crystals of table salt are made of sodium and chlorine atoms. Ice crystals, or snowflakes, are made of hydrogen and oxygen atoms.

This jewellery features many stunning diamond crystals and one very large sapphire crystal. Diamond contains only carbon atoms, while sapphire contains aluminium and oxygen atoms with a little bit of iron or titanium mixed in.

Big crystals and small crystals

The diamonds, sapphires and rubies you see in rings, necklaces and other jewellery are all examples of large, beautiful crystals.

WHAT A DISCOVERY!

In 1772, a French scientist named Rome de l'Isle worked out that the atoms inside a crystal are arranged in units that stack together in a regular way.

Not all crystals are the size of the diamonds you see in jewellery, however. For example, the crystals that make up the **minerals** feldspar and chalcedony are usually very small.

Minerals

A mineral is a natural solid material with a specific chemical makeup and structure that never changes. This means that they always look the same, both inside and outside. Some rocks are made of just one kind of mineral, but most contain from two to ten minerals. Slate is a rock that is sometimes used to make roof or floor tiles. It usually contains the minerals mica, quartz and pyrite. Each of these minerals contains crystals.

DID YOU KNOW?

Pyrite is not the only mineral that contains iron and sulfur. Chalcopyrite (left) is made up of iron, sulfur and copper atoms. People often mine chalcopyrite and heat it to remove the copper crystals. Then they use the copper to make things, such as water pipes or electricity wires.

5

Seven kinds of crystals

You probably see table salt every day, but have you ever looked at it really closely? If you did, you would see that each tiny crystal of salt is shaped like a cube. Crystals of the **minerals** galena and fluorite are also cube-shaped.

Crystal shapes

Not all crystals are shaped like cubes. If you look at a calcite crystal, you will see that it looks different from a crystal of salt. A calcite crystal is hexagonal. Crystals of ice and graphite are also hexagonal. Most crystals have one of seven different shapes, which are shown in the illustration on the next page. A crystal's shape and the location of its sides can help scientists to identify which crystal they are looking at.

DID YOU KNOW?

Hundreds of years ago, table salt was as valuable as gold is today. In some parts of the world, people used salt, just like money, to buy and sell things. This is where the word 'salary' comes from. Why was salt worth so much? Before refrigeration, salt was needed to dry out meat and other foods to preserve them for future use.

Scientists who study crystals are called **crystallographers**. A Danish physician named Nicolaus Steno (1638–1686) may have been the world's first crystallographer. He recognized that the **faces** of the same kinds of crystals are always at the same angles. Today, crystallographers have a special way of 'seeing' what a crystal's inner structure looks like. They use high-powered electron microscopes to photograph the shadows and reflections of the crystal's **atoms**. Crystallographers can then use this information to figure out how the atoms are arranged.

Nearly all crystals have one of these seven shapes.

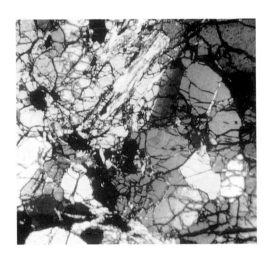

This is what an olivine crystal looks like through an electron microscope. Light microscopes can magnify objects up to 2000 times, but an electron microscope can magnify objects as much as a million times.

SEE FOR YOURSELF

It may seem hard to believe, but even though every ice crystal is hexagonal, no two snowflakes are identical. Each one is a little different from the rest. To see this for yourself, put a piece of black sugar paper in the freezer and wait for the next time it snows. Catch some snowflakes on the cold black paper and then look at each one carefully with a hand lens before they melt.

It's a habit

A habit is something you do regularly. Some people have a habit of wearing particular clothes or saying certain words. Other people have a habit of chewing gum.

Believe it or not, crystals have habits, too. Under the right conditions a **mineral** can form a large, beautiful crystal. Then the crystal's habit – its shape on the outside – has the same regular, repeating pattern as the **atoms** inside it.

Crystal flowers

Outside forces, such as heat or pressure, sometimes prevent a crystal from developing normally. Then its habit may look more like a blossoming flower, a religious cross, or even a blob. Gypsum often forms beautiful crystals, but

DID YOU KNOW?

If a tiny piece of rock or another material lands on a crystal as it is forming, the crystal may be affected. Sometimes you have to look at the crystal through a microscope to see the difference. In other cases, the particle can make a very big difference. When brownish-yellow, needle-like crystals of titanium oxide form inside a crystal of quartz, the result is called 'maiden hair'.

under some conditions it has a flower-shaped habit called 'desert rose'.

Twinning

Sometimes one crystal grows against or through another crystal in a process called **twinning**. Staurolite, aragonite and pyroxene can all form twins. Some twinned crystals have alternating colours.

Crystals of aragonite are often long and brittle. Sometimes they intersect and grow together, forming a cross-shaped structure.

Gypsum and obsidian

When the atoms in gypsum are arranged in a solid mass, it is called alabaster. Because alabaster is soft and easy to carve, it is often used to make vases or small sculptures. Obsidian is a shiny, black mass. It forms quickly as the lava it is made from cools and hardens after contact with water or air. Obsidian, therefore, does not have time to form crystals.

Crystals can form in water

Such large, beautiful crystals are very rare. They form only in places that remain undisturbed for long periods of time.

When materials dissolved in a liquid, such as water, join together and form a solid material, crystals often grow. The **atoms** may join together because the water cools down or because some of the water **evaporates**.

Large crystals of the mineral calcite often form near hot springs. Crystals of the minerals quartz, galena, fluorite and barite form when hot waters flow through rock deep below the Earth's surface.

Caves

The beautiful travertine crystals that make up stalactites in some caves form when water drips from the ceiling of a cave. The water then evaporates, leaving behind a tiny deposit.

IMAGINE THAT!

Have you ever noticed a hard, white material slowly building up inside an electric kettle? That material is made up of calcium carbonate crystals left behind when water evaporated to form steam.

Over time, the crystals slowly build up. The stalagmites that grow up from the floor of some caves form in the same way. Other beautiful structures found in caves form as crystals of calcite and gypsum slowly build up over time.

Borax crystals contain atoms of boron, sodium and oxygen. Natural borax deposits are found in USA, Chile, Germany and Italy.

Salt and borax

The crystals of two minerals we use every day – salt and borax – formed millions of years ago when ancient seas and lakes dried up. Today, salt is mined from land that was once covered by salty seas. Crystals of borax formed as the water in ancient lakes slowly evaporated. Today, we use borax to keep our clothes clean and bright and to make heavy, durable glass that can be used to make containers for baking bread, cakes and pies.

Crystals can form in magma

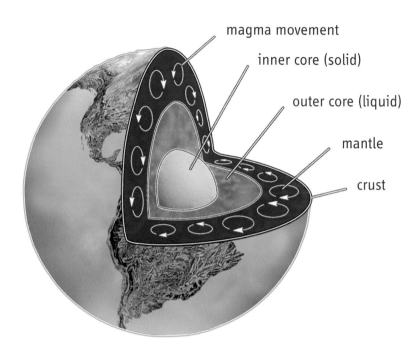

magma movement

inner core (solid)

outer core (liquid)

mantle

crust

The Earth is made up of layers. The thin outer layer of the Earth is the crust. The next layer, the mantle, is made of magma that is constantly moving. The core is made of an outer liquid layer and an inner solid core.

Below the Earth's thin crust is a layer 2900 kilometres (1800 miles) thick called the **mantle**. The mantle is made of hot, liquid rock, known as **magma**. At the Earth's centre is a sizzling hot **core**. Believe it or not, some parts of that core are hotter than the surface of the Sun.

Heat and pressure

Heat energy from the core is always moving into the mantle. All that energy forces the molten magma to churn constantly within the mantle. Once in a while, magma finds a crack in the Earth's crust and travels all the way to the surface to spill onto the land through a **volcano**. Then the hot, flowing material is called lava. As the lava quickly cools, tiny crystals of the minerals feldspar, pyroxene and olivine may grow to form basalt, phonolite, andesite and other kinds of volcanic rock.

Not all escaping magma makes it to the Earth's surface, however. Pools of magma can be trapped at some depth underground. This magma cools much more slowly than lava and forms larger crystals, which can grow slowly over thousands of years.

Weathering

These valuable crystals come to the Earth's surface only when all the surrounding volcanic rock is slowly broken down and worn away. At the same time that magma is cooling to create new rock, other forces on the Earth's surface are working to destroy existing rock. Over time, wind and water can **erode** even the toughest rock. Rocks can also be broken down by creatures in the soil, by plant roots and by repeated freezing and thawing. This process is called **weathering**.

Because many of the most valuable crystals are very hard, they can stand up to erosion and weathering. That is why sapphires, rubies, diamonds and emeralds are often found left behind in the sandy material that forms on riverbeds or in gravel when a stream or river changes its course.

After lava explodes out of a volcano, such as Kilauea on the island of Hawaii, it cools and hardens to form igneous rock. Because air cools lava quickly, volcanic rock usually contains very small crystals.

Gems and gemstones

A **gemstone** is a mineral that is rare and beautiful. It must also be durable (strong and hard) enough to wear as jewellery. After a mineral is cut and polished, it is called a **gem** or a jewel.

Topaz, tourmaline, garnet, alexandrite and peridot are all beautiful and durable gemstones. They are called 'semi-precious' because they are less rare and relatively inexpensive.

Sapphires, rubies and emeralds are all precious gemstones. They are rare, so they cost a lot of money. Diamonds are the most prized gemstones of all. Diamond is the hardest mineral on the Earth, and it sparkles with a fiery brilliance.

Sulfur is a mineral with beautiful crystals, but it is not a gemstone. It is not hard enough, so it scratches too easily to be made into jewellery.

The value of a cut gemstone is based on its beauty, rarity, hardness and how it has been cut and polished. A gem cutter will choose a shape to best display the unique qualities of the stone.

DID YOU KNOW?

Gems are measured in carats. The word 'carat' comes from a Greek word meaning 'carob bean'. One carat weighs about 0.2 gram – about as much as one of the seeds inside a carob bean.

Gemstone to jewel

Once a gemstone has been cut and polished the jewel can look stunning. That's because gem cutters know a few tricks.

Over hundreds of years, people have learned how to grind the edges of a gemstone so that it sparkles as much as possible. Today, most gemstones are cut with special tools that have blades made of ground diamonds.

Reflecting light

Creating the perfect combination of angled cuts, or **facets**, takes hours of patient work. After a gemstone is cut, light enters each facet and is reflected around inside before shooting back out. The cut gives the gem its fiery brilliance.

One of the most important centres for cutting precious stones is the Netherlands, particularly the cities of Amsterdam and Antwerp. Hong Kong and South Africa are also famous for their expert cutters.

THAT'S INCREDIBLE!

Corundum (above, with embedded ruby) is a colourless mineral with crystals made of aluminium and oxygen **atoms**. Just a few chromium atoms turn the mineral into a brilliant red ruby. When a little iron and titanium sneaks into the crystals, corundum becomes a beautiful blue sapphire.

Six of the most popular ways to cut a gem are shown below. From left to right, they are emerald cut, round brilliant, pear-shaped brilliant, cabochon, table and heart-shaped brilliant.

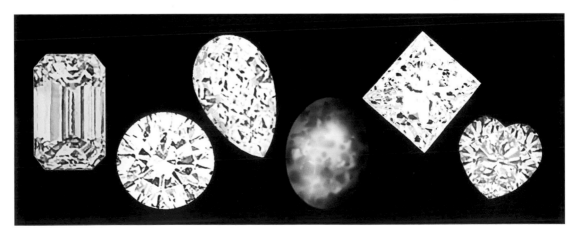

All about diamonds

These rough diamonds are shown with a measuring instrument. They are of excellent quality and will be used in jewellery.

Diamond is one of the most valuable **minerals**. In many countries, diamonds are a symbol of everlasting love. That is why many people buy diamond engagement rings. Diamonds are also popular in other kinds of jewellery. The quality of a diamond **gem** depends on its colour, clarity, size and how it has been cut.

Diamond gems can be very expensive, so you might be surprised to hear that diamonds are not rare. In fact, more than ten tonnes of diamonds are mined every year. But only about 30 per cent of all diamonds have the qualities needed to make beautiful gems. The rest are used as industrial diamonds. Because the carbon **atoms** that make up a diamond's crystal structure are tightly packed, the mineral is very hard. This makes it perfect for cutting other objects in many manufacturing processes (see page 21).

Kimberlite

Most diamonds form in a kind of **igneous rock** called kimberlite. The rock is named after the town of Kimberley, South Africa, the site of the world's deepest diamond mine. While most of the world's diamonds come from South Africa, they can also be found in other parts of Africa and in Brazil, Australia, India and Russia.

Diamonds in sand

In 1905, Frederick Wells found a fist-sized diamond in South Africa. A few years later, thousands of diamonds were found scattered on the ground in a desert area in Namibia, in southern Africa. Because the minerals had been exposed to many years of wear and tear, only the best quality diamonds had not been broken down into sand. As a result, nearly all of the diamonds found there could be used to make beautiful gems. This was one of the most impressive diamond finds of all time.

This diamond is embedded in kimberlite, an igneous rock. Most diamonds are found in kimberlite that forms deep below the Earth's surface.

WHAT A HISTORY!

Because diamonds are so valuable, the history of many large diamonds has been carefully recorded. The history of the famous Koh-i-noor diamond can be traced back more than 5000 years. For centuries, it was passed from one Indian ruler to the next. But when the Muslims conquered India in 1526, the diamond became the property of the Mongol ruler, Babur. It was stolen from his grandson and eventually returned to Indian control. In 1849, British soldiers discovered the fiery gem and sent it to Queen Victoria as a gift.

Synthetic gemstones

Natural crystals form slowly over thousands to millions of years. That is why people have been searching for ways to imitate and make crystals for at least 3600 years. At first, people tried to pass off rock crystal as diamond. They used spinel and garnet to imitate ruby. Citrine, a kind of yellow quartz, was said to be topaz, and topaz was sold as yellow sapphire.

At one time, spinel (above) and garnet (below) were used to imitate rubies. Both crystals come in many different colours, depending on the **atoms** they contain.

Natural versus artificial

Although the equipment used to make artificial crystals is expensive, **synthetic** crystals still cost 10 to 100 times less than the real thing. A 45-kilogram batch of cubic zirconia costs only a few US dollars per carat. And while natural crystals are often flawed, artificial crystals are usually perfect. They can also be made in any size or shape.

The first real success in the effort to make artificial **gemstones** came in 1837, when a French scientist named Marc Gauder grew some artificial rubies in his lab. But he only managed to make flakes, not large crystals. In 1902, Antoine Vereuil, a scientist working at the Museum of Natural History in Paris, France, perfected a technique for making artificial rubies. It worked so well that we still use Vereuil's method today. A similar process is used to make artificial sapphires, spinels, emeralds and other gemstones.

Making diamonds

In 1954, H. Tracy Hall, a scientist working at a research lab in the state of New York in the USA, discovered a way to make artificial diamonds that could be used for industrial purposes. He later said that when he realized his success, 'My hands began to tremble; my heart beat rapidly; my knees weakened and no longer gave support. My eyes had caught the flashing light … and I knew that diamonds had finally been made by man.' Today, Hall's process is used to make nearly 20,000 kilograms of artificial diamonds every year.

DID YOU KNOW?

Today's favourite diamond look-alike is cubic zirconia, which is made from superheated sand. Only an expert can tell the difference between a cubic zirconia and a diamond. A cubic zirconia crystal is the same colour as a diamond and even sparkles like a diamond, but a diamond is harder and more durable.

How do people use crystals?

You now know that crystals of many **minerals** are cut to create the sparkling **gems** used in jewellery, religious objects and pieces of art. But crystals are also used in many other ways.

We eat crystals of salt every day. It adds flavour to the food. Salt can also be used to preserve food for long periods of time and to melt the ice on roads in winter. Crystals of epsomite are the main ingredient in epsom salts. Dissolved in bath water, epsom salts clean cuts and reduce swelling. Quartz crystals are used to make the microchips that run our computers and keep our watches running.

This tiny, square microchip could not be made without quartz. Almost all microchips are made from silicon, the chief component of quartz.

When people look through a crystal of Iceland spar – a kind of calcite – they see two of everything. That's because when rays of light pass through this crystal, they separate and create a double image. This quality makes calcite crystals the perfect choice for use in some types of microscopes.

Hard and sharp

About 70 per cent of the diamonds mined are not of high enough quality to be used as gems, but they are still useful. Because diamonds are so hard, they are perfect for making dentists' drills, drill bits for oil wells and special scalpels for very delicate medical operations. Diamonds also carry sound and light waves well, so they are used in hearing aids, transmitters that carry telephone and television signals and equipment used to locate fish and submarines in the ocean. Because diamonds can tolerate extreme heat and cold, they have also been used to make the windows in some spacecraft and satellites.

Corundum

Corundum is second only to diamond in hardness. Corundum crystals are used to grind and polish a variety of objects, including softer **gemstones**. They are also used to make emery paper and emery boards for filing fingernails.

This view through an electron microscope shows the diamond fragments on the tip of a dentist's drill. Diamonds make excellent drill material because they are the hardest mineral on the Earth.

DID YOU KNOW?

The word 'crystal' comes from a Greek term meaning 'icy cold'. The ancient Greeks believed that rock crystal, a kind of colourless quartz, was made of ice that had frozen so hard it would never thaw.

Where on Earth are crystals?

Within the Earth's tallest mountains, below its widest plains and underneath its seabeds, lie a multitude of large and small crystals. Many of the largest and most prized crystals form in **igneous rock**. Igneous rock can be mined from underground or exposed to the surface as wind and water slowly break down and remove the rock above it.

DID YOU KNOW?

The Logan sapphire, the largest blue sapphire ever discovered, was found in Sri Lanka. The gem weighs 765 grams and is on display at the Smithsonian Institution in Washington, D.C., USA.

Giant crystals

At Etta Mine near Keystone, in the US state of South Dakota, miners found a pale-green crystal of spodumene that was as big as a house and weighed nearly 90 tonnes. But that was nothing compared to what workers discovered near Karrelia in Russia. The giant feldspar crystals found there weighed thousands of tonnes each.

This rare yellow sapphire was discovered in Sri Lanka. In Sri Lanka, sapphire and other gemstones are often found among sandy **sediments** in rivers and streams.

Sri Lanka, an island country off the southeast tip of India, is sometimes called **Gem** Island. It has rich deposits of alexandrite, ruby, sapphire, topaz, garnet, spinel and tourmaline. While some of the **gemstones** are mined, many can be found among pebbles **eroded** from larger rocks by heavy rains.

Crystals in gravel

A large area of granite in northeast Brazil is also rich in gemstones. As the area was folded and uplifted by forces deep within the Earth, the rock was brought to the surface. As heavy rains in the region slowly break down the granite, huge piles of gravel containing beautiful crystals of topaz, diamond, emerald, aquamarine and tourmaline are left behind.

Emerald is a form of a colourless mineral called beryl. Just a few **atoms** of chromium give emerald its brilliant green colour.

WHAT A DISCOVERY!

Some of the most valuable sapphires are mined from rock at Yogo Gulch in the American state of Montana. Gemstones were first discovered there in the late 1800s by a gold prospector named Jack Hoover. During a hailstorm, Hoover took shelter under a ledge. To pass the time, he scraped away some of the rock and later examined it to see if it contained any gold. The rock contained a little gold along with some small blue crystals. He sent the blue stones to an old girlfriend who lived in Maine. When she wrote to thank him for 'the sapphires', Hoover realized that he had found something more valuable than gold and opened a mine.

23

Crystal powers

Crystals have fascinated people for thousands of years. The ancient Greeks and Romans thought fortune-tellers could see future events in crystal balls made of quartz. Some people believed that a diamond increased a person's strength, a peridot gave a person dignity and an opal brought love and hope.

In ancient times, some people placed emeralds under their tongues. They believed this would give them the power to predict the future.

Power and wisdom

In some cultures, rubies symbolized power and romance. Others claimed that the brilliant red stone could cure diseases of the liver or spleen. Some people said the sapphire made a foolish person wise, but Roman Catholic priests often wore sapphire rings to symbolize their purity. Many soldiers were convinced that amethyst would keep them safe during battles and garnets would heal their wounds more quickly.

Sailors in some parts of the world believed that aquamarines brought them good luck at sea. Long ago, Native Americans belonging to the Navajo tribe would throw turquoise into the

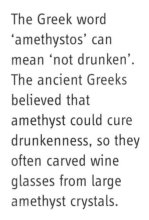

river and say a prayer when they wanted it to rain.

Healing

Some people still believe that crystals have special powers. At Crystal Academy in Taos, in the US state of New Mexico, students learn the art of crystal healing. The teachers there believe that when a person's body absorbs energy from the crystals, he or she will heal more quickly.

For almost 2000 years, people have called certain objects 'birthstones', but people did not begin to wear birthstones as jewellery until the 1700s. Most of the birthstones are crystals, but a few are not. A pearl is a not a crystal. It is made by an oyster secreting the mineral aragonite. An opal is sometimes called a '**gem**', but it is made of tiny ball-shaped grains, not crystals. Turquoise is a rock made of many minerals.

The Greek word 'amethystos' can mean 'not drunken'. The ancient Greeks believed that amethyst could cure drunkenness, so they often carved wine glasses from large amethyst crystals.

BIRTHSTONES BY MONTH

MONTH	BIRTHSTONE
January	Garnet
February	Amethyst
March	Aquamarine
April	Diamond
May	Emerald
June	Pearl
July	Ruby
August	Peridot
September	Sapphire
October	Opal
November	Topaz
December	Turquoise

Crystal gallery

Most of the crystals that make up minerals are so small that you need a microscope to see them. But under the correct conditions they sometimes grow quite large and can be incredibly beautiful. Some of the most dazzling crystals are on display at museums around the world.

Topaz crystals can be yellow, red, blue, green or colourless. Yellow-orange topaz gemstones are often used to make jewellery.

Topaz

Topaz is a semi-precious **gem** that is usually golden brown, but it may also be colourless, pink or pale blue. Stunning topaz crystals have been found in Russia and Brazil. The Brazilian Princess, the second largest topaz in the world, weighs 4.5 kilograms and is the size of a car's headlamp. During a two-year process, it was cut from a 11.8-kilogram **gemstone**.

The Hope diamond

Most diamonds are colourless, but the Hope diamond is a deep blue colour. The diamond's colour comes from a little bit of boron mixed in with the carbon **atoms**. At one time, people believed that this magnificent jewel brought bad luck to whoever owned it.

The Hope diamond was found in India. Over the years it has had many owners, including King Louis XIV of France. Today, the Hope diamond is on display at the Smithsonian Institution in Washington, D.C., USA. Many other large, impressive diamonds have also been found in South Africa.

Geodes and nodules

A **geode** is a round mass of rock that has a hollow cavity lined with large crystals. Most geodes contain crystals of the minerals quartz or calcite.

A **nodule** is a round mass of rock completely filled with small crystals of agate, jasper or chalcedony.

Both geodes and nodules are most often found within the rock formed from volcanic lava that cooled quickly. They began as large air bubbles in the lava or, more rarely, as animal burrows, tree roots or mud balls swept up by the lava.

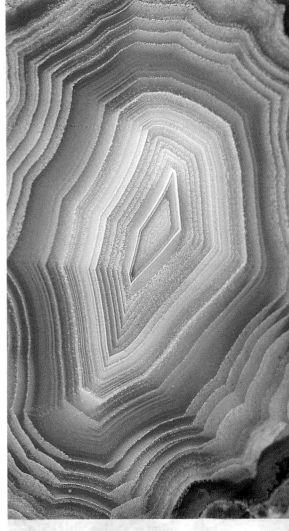

DID YOU KNOW?

Some minerals can have different kinds of crystals depending on how quickly they cool. Agate (above), jasper, chalcedony, amethyst, smoky quartz and citrine are all forms of quartz. Crystals of agate, jasper and chalcedony form quickly and are small. Amethyst, smoky quartz and citrine have larger crystals because they cool more slowly.

A closer look at crystals

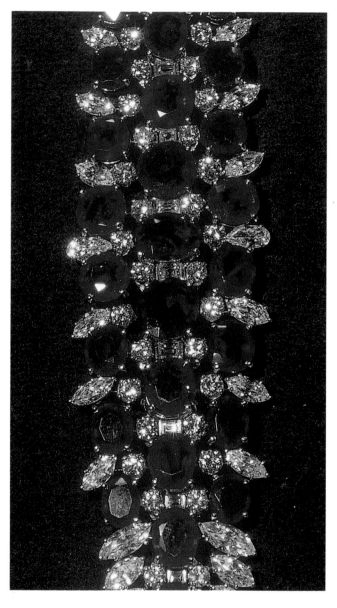

A jewellery shop is a good place to find crystals like these rubies and diamonds. You are not likely to find them in nature.

Now that you know all about crystals, you may want to get a closer look at some yourself. One of the best places to start is at a local jewellery shop. You will be able to see many beautiful **gems**, including diamonds, sapphires, rubies, amethysts and peridots.

Crystals in museums

If you'd like to see some lovely crystals of minerals that are not durable enough to wear as jewellery, visit a natural history museum or attend a mineral show in your area. The people selling the minerals won't mind if you look at their samples, but make sure don't touch them unless you intend to buy them.

Crystal hunting

You could even try hunting for large, beautiful crystals near your home. You probably won't find diamonds or emeralds, but you may be able to spot some quartz crystals.

Quartz is the most common mineral on the Earth's surface and you can see quartz crystals in many rocks or washed up on rocky beaches. If you decide to hunt for crystals in nature, you will need to learn a few simple rules. You may also need to gather together some basic equipment.

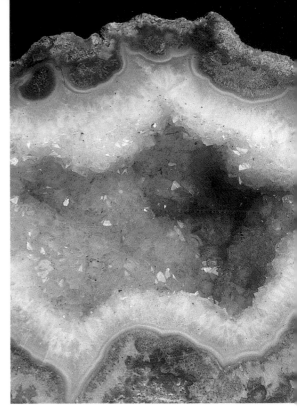

The **geode** is the official state rock of the US state of Iowa. Geodes can also be found in many other places. The layers of crystals inside a geode are formed when minerals in the rock cavity dissolve in water.

WHAT YOU NEED TO KNOW

- Never look for crystals on your own. Go with a group that includes a qualified adult.
- Know how to use a map and compass.
- Always get a landowner's permission before walking on private property. If you find some rocks with interesting crystals, ask if you can take them home with you.
- Before removing samples from public land, make sure collecting is allowed. Many natural rock formations are protected by law.
- Respect nature. Do not hammer out samples. Do not disturb living things and do not leave litter.

WHAT YOU NEED

- Strong boots or wellies
- A map and compass
- A small paintbrush to remove dirt and extra rock and mineral chips from samples
- A camera to take photographs of rock and mineral formations
- A hand lens to get a close-up look at crystals
- A notebook for recording when and where you find each rock
- A spotter's guide to rocks and minerals.

Glossary

atom smallest unit of an element that still has all the properties of the element

core centre of the Earth. The inner core is solid, and the outer core is liquid.

crust outer layer of the Earth

crystallographer scientist who studies crystals

erode to slowly wear away rock over time by the action of wind, water or glaciers

evaporate to change from a liquid to a gas

face smooth, flat side of a crystal

facet angled cut a gem cutter makes to bring out a gem's beauty

gem beautiful mineral that has been cut and polished

gemstone beautiful mineral that may be worn as jewellery

geode round mass of rock that has a hollow cavity lined with large crystals

igneous rock kind of rock that forms when magma from the Earth's mantle cools and hardens

magma hot, liquid rock that makes up the Earth's mantle. When magma spills out onto the Earth's surface, it is called lava.

mantle layer of the Earth between the crust and outer core. It is made of rock in a liquid form, known as magma.

mineral natural solid material with a specific chemical makeup and structure

nodule round mass of rock completely filled with small crystals

sediment mud, clay or bits of rock picked up by rivers and streams and dumped in the ocean

synthetic man-made

twinning one crystal growing against or through another crystal

volcano opening in the Earth's surface that extends into the mantle

weathering breaking down of rock by plant roots or by repeated freezing and thawing

Further information

BOOKS

The best book of fossils, rocks and minerals, Chris Pellant, Kingfisher, 2000

Collecting gems and minerals, Chris Pellant, David and Charles, 1999

The eyewitness guide to crystals and gems, R F Symes, Dorling Kindersley, 2000

The Kingfisher book of planet Earth, Martin Redfern, Kingfisher, 1999

The pebble in my pocket, Meredith Hopper, Frances Lincoln, 1997

Tourists rock, fossil and mineral map of Great Britain, British Geological Survey, 2000

ORGANIZATIONS

British Geological Survey
www.bgs.ac.uk
Kingsley Dunham Centre, Keyworth, Nottingham, NG12 5GG UK

Rockwatch
www.geologist.demon.co.uk/rockwatch/
The Geologists' Association
Burlington House, Piccadilly, London, W1V 9AG UK

The Natural History Museum
www.nhm.ac.uk
Cromwell Road,
London, SW7 5BD UK

The Geological Society of Australia
www.gsa.org.au/home
Suite 706, 301 George Street
Sydney NSW
Australia 2000

Geological Survey of Canada
www.nrcan.gc.ca/gsc/
601 Booth Street
Ottawa, Ontario
KIA 0E8
Canada

US Geological Survey (USGS)
www.usgs.gov
507 National Center
12201 Sunrise Valley Drive
Reston, Virginia 22092
USA

Index

Titles in the *Rocks and Minerals* series include:

Hardback   0 431 14370 6

Hardback   0 431 14371 4

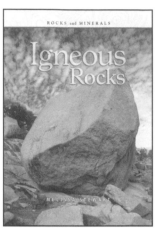

Hardback   0 431 14372 2

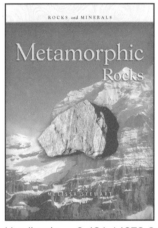

Hardback   0 431 14373 0

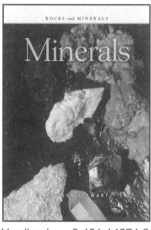

Hardback   0 431 14374 9

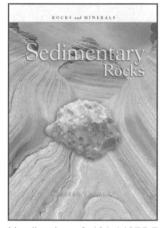

Hardback   0 431 14375 7

Hardback   0 431 14376 5

Find out about the other titles in this series on our website www.heinemann.co.uk/library